The Weeds

The Weeds

Poems by

Lynn Fanok

© 2025 Lynn Fanok. All rights reserved.
This material may not be reproduced in any form, published,
reprinted, recorded, performed, broadcast,
rewritten or redistributed without
the explicit permission of Lynn Fanok.
All such actions are strictly prohibited by law.

Cover design by Shay Culligan
Cover image by Jenna Barton
Author photo by David S. Elliman

ISBN: 978-1-63980-794-9
Library of Congress Control Number: 2025945660

Kelsay Books
502 South 1040 East, A-119
American Fork, Utah 84003
Kelsaybooks.com

"Like the dead-seeming, cold rocks, I have memories within that came out of the material that went to make me. Time and place have had their say."

—Zora Neale Hurston, *Dust Tracks on a Road*

Acknowledgments

Grateful acknowledgments are made to the editors of the following publications where versions of these poems first appeared:

Gossamer Arts: A Literary Magazine: "Borders"

Pictura Journal: "Elementary"

Red Wolf Journal: "Each of Us Plows"

Scholastic Magazine: "Fluffy White Goat"

Schuylkill Valley Journal: "Two Mamas"

I wish to extend my gratitude to the Bucks County writing community, including Ethel Rackin, Luray Gross, Joanne Leva, and Stalwarts group for their gifts of friendship and support. And a special thank-you to Judith Lagana for her optimism and valuable insights.

I would also like to express my sincere appreciation of the late poet and teacher Christopher Bursk for inspiring me—still.

Thanks to Karen Kelsay and her staff at Kelsay Books.

An additional thank-you to Newtown Bookshop owner, Kathy Morrison, for providing the space and time to hold our monthly poetry series.

And finally, thanks to *Scholastic Magazine* for encouraging creative writing at an early age, and choosing my poetic ditty as the winner of one of their limerick contests.

Love to David, always.

Contents

Each of Us Plows   13

I

The Clay Pits   17
Until Wantonness Wanes   18
Brush Fires   19
The Dirt Road   20
Elementary   21
A Bowl of Mashed Potatoes   22
Two Mamas   23
Raggedy Ann   24
The Three   25
At Home in the Weeds   26
After School at Nanna's   27

II

Out of the Blue   31
Innocence   32
Living Room of the Lost   33
After a Sweet Sixteen Party   34
Dan's Release   35
Upon Finding a Cicada Husk   36
Undone   37
Poncho   38

III

Encounter	41
Never-Ending Anxiety	42
Haunt	43
Borders	44
It Was as If Rain Chose Our Street to Rave On	45
A Mighty Oak	46

IV

The Weeds	49
Building a Bridge	50
Requiem for a Toad	51
Ephemerals	52
Snake and Toad	53
Sanctuary	54
Between Waiting and Wanting	55

Epilogue

Summer School	59

Each of Us Plows

We toil and tear at the earth:
ever amending, turning it over.

We yell at clouds of rutted truths,
at the wheat in the fields fortifying
the millstones secured to our necks.
We—the coarse grain.

I

The Clay Pits

I mined clay for a grade school project.
Dug into earth to collect enough to sculpt
representations of human evolution.

I created heads of Neanderthal, Cro-Magnon,
Homo erectus, Homo habilis. Lined them up
on the classroom table in proper ascending order.
Neanderthal, my favorite.

The social studies project inspired thoughts
of becoming an archeologist, got me interested
in fossils, rocks, plants.

The brick factory opened in the 1800s, closed in 1970.
I'd often heard locals referring to *the clay pits*.
My dad gave me driving lessons on its vacant lot.

Today, the water storage tower remains—
a slumbering monolith overlooking the marshes.

Until Wantonness Wanes

Sudden winds approach,
egg on a fiery feeding
of fields that rise

in plumes of oriole,
in plumes of cardinal.
Blackened, they fall.

Curls of serpentine smoke,
feathery ash, drift to noses, throats,
eyelashes.

A white-hot glow reignites the burn
of wantonness that wanes.

I try to imagine fields echoing
the light of gold finches.

Brush Fires

Was it intentional?
A cigarette flicked again
from careless fingertips?

Sharp odors on the wind.
Families walked from blocks away;
spread over backyards.

Spellbound by the spectacle
of the flaming field.

The Dirt Road

Our only safeguard—a dirt road
separating us from the blaze.

It could possibly, would surely,
foil fire.

rock, paper, scissors—
could it?

rock, paper, scissors—
would it?

rock, paper, scissors—

Having no choice, we'd wait out fires
yet to come, real or imagined.

The wildness around us
was not going anywhere.

Elementary

I have a recurring dream of riding my bike
past your house, you sitting cross-legged
on your porch.

I wave, drop my bike. We string a cat's cradle,
sing pat-a-cake rhymes, weave chain bracelets
from red clover.

It was your idea to pledge our friendship
by sharing a stick of bubble gum
you pulled from your mouth.

In this dream, we play hide the thimble.
I search room after room. Find you
hidden in plain sight.

A Bowl of Mashed Potatoes

It's her birthday, and this
is what she has requested.

A huge bowl is placed
on the kitchen table.

I'm there, too, to witness
this affirmation of motherly love
fashioned from humble spuds.

*Peel the skins until what lies beneath
is revealed.*

Boil them in a tall pot.

*Mash them well—no lumps, add butter
and salt, top with rich gravy.*

Eat until warmth consumes you.

Walking home, I savor our happiness,
the afterglow.

Two Mamas

*Snapping turtles evolved around 90 million years ago.
Homo sapiens have existed less than 300,000 years.*

I imagine she'd traveled a long way
from the river's bank.

We children were curious about the menacing creature
with an oversized shell and spiked tail.

What was she up to?

She chose a spot behind our porch to deposit her eggs.
Her robust legs and claws began thrusting aside

mounds of dirt with wide, deliberate strokes.
Mom ran for a broom to nudge her away

from where we played. The mama turtle
snapped at the broom handle, kept digging.

Raggedy Ann

I envied you for having her to place on your bed,
to hug when you had trouble falling asleep.

Did you squeeze her tight to your chest, tuck her into
your flight of fancy suitcase, run away to the dark side
of the moon?

While you drifted to sleep, Raggedy Ann was awake
galloping around the room on your hobby horse, rousing
other dolls from your toy box to play and sing.

> There once was a fluffy white goat,
> Who danced on the edge of a boat,
> He did a flip-flop
> And fell on his top
> Tearing his polka dot coat.

Your eyelids twitched in time, your lips curled into a smile,
as you listened to the lilt of the lullaby.

The Three

Our friend Trish stumbled upon them
in the weeds beyond her house.

She ran home to tell.
She told Wanda and me,
. . . near the river . . .
inside plastic bags.

I told my mom.
She told me,
Don't go in the weeds.
Don't.

Did I listen?
Of course not.

At Home in the Weeds

They swayed golden, waist high,
gently brushing my legs in summertime.

Filled with mystery, threats, promise:
fires, floods, death, regrowth, play.

What will I discover today?

Ant hills. A nubby toad.
Squash ripe purple pokeweed berries.

A dragonfly hovers—
zips away.

Feather soft soil sifts
through my fingers.

Prickly stickers plucked
from socks and sleeves.

Dinnertime, I run home, eager
to tell mom everything.

After School at Nanna's

We dashed up the stairs to reach
the screened-in porch.

Nanna's hair swirled in a bun,
cinnamon, with white frosting.

She brought us coffee cake juniors
and fruit punch on a tray.

We pecked at the sweet crumbles
like swamp sparrows.

We counted people and cars passing by
until it was dinnertime.

Nanna's plump cat, Snowy, lazed
on the sundrenched driveway.

She gave us a quick *mew*, a wide yawn
revealing pointy fangs.

Across the street, wild turkeys
squawking in the tall grasses.

A flash of white. Snowy gone.

II

Out of the Blue

Pre-teens, we were dropped off
at Brunswick Square Mall.

We admired gold and silver necklaces,
bangles, earrings, glittering under lights.

The dazzling display of gemstones,
the stuff of pirate treasures.

As we headed out of the store,
a security guard stopped us.

I was baffled until a smirk
appeared on Wanda's lips.

The guard ushered us to a back office.
He offered Wanda a cigarette.

Before we left, she confessed
to pocketing a charm bracelet.

Wanda, who soon after, painted
her bedroom walls and ceiling
midnight blue.

Innocence

Why?
Because he was a gentle, lanky boy
with a lumbering gait

and a bit of a stoop, who kept
his head to the ground,

who didn't dare lift or look up,
fearful of what would fall out.

Because he'd dug up arrowheads
for show-and-tell.

He couldn't stop tripping over his tongue.
Snickers from classmates, a stain of shame.

Because in his room he cared for small green turtles
with bits of lettuce strewn about.

Because he'd explain how to spot guppies
or tadpoles in ponds.

The newspapers said, *Detectives searched the weeds . . .
knocked on all our doors . . . investigation ongoing . . .*

No, he didn't. He couldn't have.

Living Room of the Lost

Mr. Dambrowski sat on his couch, TV off,
staring out his living room window.

He had lost a finger at the plant.
Was placed on permanent disability.

He was indifferent to me and Wanda.
Not wishing to disturb him, we always
walked past without saying a word.

No longer working, my own father stood
with faraway eyes, shoulders slouched,
at our living room window.

Asks if I would stop by the liquor store
for a six-pack.

After a Sweet Sixteen Party

Balloons bobbing freely in the backseat
of her Honda Civic.

I park my Pontiac Ventura in my usual spot.
Run inside. Less than five minutes—BANG!

I hear an eerie whirring. See my car thrust
across the street. Its undercarriage scrapes

the neighbor's curb. Lands on their front lawn.
Scents of oil and smoke waft from under its hood.

A stream of red runs from the driver's nose,
Jack Daniel's on her breath.

A neighbor rushes out with a towel.
She's okay. She's okay.

But, *my* car,
my car,
my very first car!

Dan's Release

I saw Mr. Dambrowski's son Dan
casually skip across the bridge
in the direction of home.

His manner, as laid-back as the Levi's
we'd beg our moms to let us buy
at Greenfield's on Main Street.

I'd heard he'd served time.
The story's details, hazy.

Was it years of mockery and bullying
that conjured a storm that led to violence?

I was puzzled by his release, wanted
to know more and now, here he was
flowing along, crossing the river, reborn.

If only he had drank from the River Lethe—
all memories, all sins, softly cleansed
in the velvety silt of the wetlands.

Upon Finding a Cicada Husk

The tambura-like drone
etched in our minds reintroduces us
to almost forgotten summer.

Sturdy forelegs propelled him
on a subterranean journey up, up,
up, to this branch, on this tree.

Eyelash length antennae droop.
Where eyes should be, there's
cellophane, transparency.

Winglets lie in repose like grief.
A single split between his shoulders
offered release.

Undone

> ... *She's gone too far / She's lost the sun* ...
> —The Guess Who, 1969

I.

Janis Joplin revisited her Texas hometown
wearing layers of hippie beads, frayed jeans,

feather boa in her hair. Did disapproving stares,
gossip from those she'd known hurt?

On the lonesome road, a void needed filling.
Gale-force howls, painful wails, a forecast.

II.

Wanda climbed onto the school bus,
her long brown hair covering half her face.

She wore a *Frampton Comes Alive* concert t-shirt,
patched jeans, armfuls of silver bangles.

She was greeted with a chorus of *Wacky Wanda*.
The nickname didn't seem a bother.

She gave a quick nod, took a seat at the back,
bummed a cigarette from a burnout.

That year, she started cutting classes, hung out
behind the gym getting high, was held after school.

Decades later, she flew too high, too low,
maybe both.

Poncho

A white rabbit from Mexico,
a gift from my dad
who built it a pen.

Sometimes, I'd bring it inside,
let it wander on my bed,
talk softly to it, secretly
wishing it would purr.

It was a gentle creature,
meant to be quiet, to not
draw attention.

I loved the tall grasses
that grew far beyond my sight
until a stray pack of dogs
appeared one night.

In the morning, signs of a frenzy,
sullied damp earth.

With foxlike curiosity, I tracked
tattered patches of fur. Death
tucked into the weeds.

III

Encounter

I remember your start.
Missed the intermission.
Heard about your end.

Dad bumped into her at Nick's Hideout.
Said she'd asked about me.
She bought him a beer.
He told her I'd found a job.

Questions I would've asked
had I been present:

How've you been?
Work? School? Married? Children?

How's life been treating you?
Are you happy?

Never-Ending Anxiety

It lingers
like an affliction,
holds your hands
in damp mittens,
while you endure—
build your snowman,
develop frostbite on fingers
that should be playing the flute.

Haunt

I'd like to go back
to our 1970s neighborhood.
Demystify what dwelled in The Weeds—
wonderful
and awful things
ascended,
descended,
in the wetlands'
grasses, reeds, rushes.

Maybe I'll go back. It's precarious though,
with the landscape being so unstable,
unpredictable.

Some lives rose
above the mire.
Some were destined
to be trapped
in its slippery clay.
Water pressure
broke up the rest.

We became part of the wetlands,
composed of minerals, plants, animals.
We, too, were washed away.

Borders

A dirt road ran like a secret
between us and the weeds.

Our homes on the edge of town,
low-lying land, a river.

Floods.
Talk of paving the dirt road.

Floods.
Talk of building more homes
beyond.

Floods.
The dirt road, the land untouched,
untamed.

It Was as If Rain Chose Our Street to Rave On

Hurricane Sandy, 2012

As children, we held bike races, played hopscotch,
ran toward the ice cream truck's tune.

For years, neighbors wrung their hands
over backed-up sewers, yard floods.

How much did it take to fill basements,
collapse cinder block walls, climb stairs?

Afterwards, our street inundated
with mud, waste, drowned rats.

Kitchen tables and chairs, saturated rugs
and mattresses heaped curbside.

We were offered a government buyout.
Homes bulldozed. Concrete driveway aprons
untouched.

Neighbors got on with living. Some relocated
to Florida. A handful of holdouts couldn't
afford to leave.

What remained?

The area had returned to its natural state.
I'm certain, if I'd lingered longer, I could've heard
the cackle of ring-necked pheasants reveling in the fields.

A Mighty Oak

My brother told me to look for you.
I returned. You, still standing.

I found you. I found you, Mighty Oak.
Your hefty torso, broad branches,
withstood raging hurricane winds.

I remember how mom watched
from the kitchen window as we sang,
*Ring around the rosie, pocket full of posies,
ashes, ashes, we all fall . . .*

You, too, were in her line of sight.
She admired your ever-changing moods.

Mom watched us play. You offered relief
from summer's sun.

*Do you know how many oaks have outlived
the humans that have planted them?
How long will you live?*

A marker of a now absent family,
you live on.

IV

The Weeds

When we were children, I followed you
through the weeds behind your house.

I looked back, saw our houses
becoming smaller and smaller.

We crushed slender stalks under our sneakers,
pushed aside reedy cattails that stood in our way

until we found what we came for—
a clearing and, within it, muskrat homes

made of mud, grasses, reeds, piled layer
upon layer, shaped into domes.

Years later, at a class reunion, your heart-shaped face
appeared on the screen, *In memoriam* . . .

I recalled where we stood so small
in the marshes, growing taller.

Building a Bridge

Mom would drive us across the bridge
to the nearby river town in her black
tail-finned Pontiac to Dairy Queen,

Stewart's Root Beer for chili dogs,
Ben Franklin's Five and Dime
to buy school supplies.

Plans were in the works for a new
overpass to replace the small,
outdated bridge.

Parents explained, it's a slow process—
foundation, substructure, superstructure.
How long? When will it be done? When?

We children occupied the wait by turning
lemons into lemonade. Gathered our sleds,
scrambled to the top of the icy slope, Wanda

dragging her red sled behind. We raced downward,
tumbling toward our joyful destination, bellies
aching with laughter.

Decades later, according to classmates,
she was found in winter underneath the bridge.

What led her to this place?

If it were possible, I'd rectify all circumstances
that shuttered her light.

Requiem for a Toad

I'm sure I saw him earlier
crouching under the downspout.

Now, his body stuck to sizzling blacktop,
mouth agape as if screaming, *HELP!*

I can see down his pink throat, slick
as a water slide.

I recall pungent formaldehyde permeating
the classroom and hall.

Frogs in tall industrial grade plastic buckets.
Innards splayed on cold metal trays.

I loosen him from the asphalt.
Dig a small hole beneath a rose bush.

Taking this small care, *Will my roses
grow stronger?*

Ephemerals

I grasp the daffodils'
faded yellow strands,
silky tresses.

They loosen, slide
through my fingers.
I barely remember their faces.

Snake and Toad

Snake does
what it was born to do.

Toad does
what it was born to do.

What defense does a toad, soft as a pillow,
hold against venom?

Sanctuary

Some live a lifetime filled with longing,
and the loneliness of knowing this will not change.
It is part of them now.

Light of the day

Preserve
Embrace
Cushion
Shelter

Between Waiting and Wanting

Sunbeams alighted on our daydreamer days
of cattails, of weedy stalks, of mud and clay.

As children, we always seemed to be
in the middle of waiting and wanting.

Our minds in the kitchen cooking up fictions:
notions of forever in our giddiness of play,
magic wands, troll dolls, a rabbit's foot on a chain.

Today, thoughts, dreams, revisit like ghosts
in the kitchen, rattling pots and pans—
I listen.

Epilogue

Summer School

I learned how to turn out dreams
    gathering Queen Anne's lace.

I learned the pleasure of sweetness
    sucking red clover.

I learned about loss
    plucking petals of dandelions.

I learned there is too much to learn
    during summer's brief time.

About the Author

Lynn Fanok was born and raised in New Jersey and has written two poetry collections that focus on aspects of her formative years. In her first book, *Bread and Fumes,* she describes her late father, a WWII Nazi labor camp survivor, and explores her Ukrainian heritage, culture, and relations. In her latest book, *The Weeds,* she writes about childhood friendships and loss, natural disasters, and restoration.

Fanok lives with her husband in Bucks County, Pennsylvania where she leads a monthly poetry series at an independent bookstore. She holds degrees in English from The Pennsylvania State University and Arcadia University.

Her poetry has appeared in *Painted Bride Quarterly, Schuylkill Valley Journal, Tiny Seed Literary Journal, Underwood Press, Red Wolf Journal, Pictura Journal, Gossamer Arts: A Literary Magazine;* the anthology *Carry Us to the Next Well* (Kelsay Books, 2021); and *A Certain Kind of Swagger, Poems: Christopher Bursk's Poetry Master Class, 2021.*

www.ingramcontent.com/pod-product-compliance
Lightning Source LLC
Chambersburg PA
CBHW071013160426
43193CB00012B/2036